The Sabbath Bus and Other Miracle Stories

Vernon Putz

All rights reserved. No part of this publication may be reproduced, distributed, or transmitted in any form or by any means, including photocopying, recording, or other electronic or mechanical methods, without the prior written permission of the publisher, except in the case of brief quotations embodied in critical reviews and certain other noncommercial uses permitted by copyright law. For permission requests, write to the publisher, TEACH Services, Inc., at the address below.

Copyright © 2021 Vernon Putz
Copyright © 2021 TEACH Services, Inc.
ISBN-13: 978-1-4796-1252-9 (Paperback)
ISBN-13: 978-1-4796-1253-6 (ePub)
Library of Congress Control Number: 2020914061

All Scripture quotations, unless otherwise indicated, are taken from the **New International Version** (NIV) Holy Bible, New International Version®, NIV® Copyright ©1973, 1978, 1984, 2011 by Biblica, Inc.® Used by permission. All rights reserved worldwide.

The Clear Word
Copyright ©2003 by Jack J. Blanco. All rights reserved.

New American Standard Bible (NASB)
Copyright © 1960, 1962, 1963, 1968, 1971, 1972, 1973, 1975, 1977, 1995 by The Lockman Foundation

New King James Version (NKJV)
Copyright © 1982 by Thomas Nelson. Used by permission. All rights reserved.

New Life Version (NLV)
Copyright © 1969, 2003 by Barbour Publishing, Inc.

Published by

www.TEACHServices.com • (800) 367-1844

Table of Contents

Preface v

1. We Are Lost 7
2. The Making of a Missionary 10
3. God's Math Is Different 13
4. Another Disappointment 15
5. The Call of Uncle Sam 18
6. Another Test of Faith 24
7. The Angel and the Boat 28
8. Carol and the Truancy 30
9. Another Miracle Baby 33
10. Japan 35
11. His Hands Are My Hands and My Hands
    Are His Hands 37
12. Medical School 39

13. The Hawaiian Health Center 43
14. A Church Plant. 47
15. Russia Calling. 49
16. The Russian Mafia 52
17. War in Town 55
18. A New Church 57
19. The Sabbath Bus 61
20. God Saved Me 64
21. Natasha 66
22. Ordination. 69
23. Burnout 71
24. The Big "C" Word 74
25. Remarriage 78
26. Retirement 82
27. Frustration Turns to Joy. 89

Preface

It was 6:04 in the morning. I awoke at 4:47 with the impression I should get up and write. I had been feeling over the last week that I should write a book on the miracles that I have experienced in my life but had kept putting that thought aside. I have never written a book. This morning when the Lord said, "Get up and write," I began to argue:

"Lord, I don't know how to write a book."

"I will help you."

"But, Lord, You know that if I get up early, I have a hard time functioning during the day."

"I can keep you awake."

"Lord, You know that my spelling and grammar is not all that good."

"I will help you."

And so it went on for the next hour until I finally gave in and pulled myself out of the cozy bed and began to write. So here we go with *The Sabbath Bus and Other Miracle Stories.* It is my hope and prayer that these short stories will bring courage and faith to those who read.

1. We Are Lost

My father loved to fish, especially in the high-altitude lakes of the Sierras in Central California. I was about eight years old when Father decided to take the family and pack into the mountains for a fishing experience. We were joined by another family, the Millers. We got a very late start as the sun was setting in the west. That was usual on a farm, as there were so many things to do before leaving. My brother, sister, and I rode in the back of the truck covered with blankets. By the time we were winding our way up the steep mountain road, we were fast asleep. Suddenly, there was a loud crash and a scraping noise. We awoke to see the horse trailer skidding sideways. The right wheel axle had broken.

The horses were unloaded and tied to the truck, and we made our way slowly up the mountain to the trailhead. We camped in the pasture for the rest of the night and started our journey the next day. At the end of the first day, we were all, including the horses, very tired. It was getting dark. We were on a narrow trail on the side of a rock that looked straight down several hundred feet. One of the pack horses began to crumble under the load. Mr. Miller, who was just in front of that horse, realized that if that animal fell, it would fall over the cliff, pulling him and his horse over also. He instinctively pulled out his knife and cut the line that held them together. The horse fell over the cliff with our two-week supply of food.

We continued our way on up the mountain until we came to a lake where we camped. Father and Mr. Miller hiked back to the base of the cliff by flashlights to see about the horse and food. Unfortunately, the horse was dead, but they managed to rescue the food.

The next morning, the sun was shining on the lake, making a reflection of the beautiful mountains and trees surrounding the lake. The air was crisp with a delightful smell of pine. Mom made a hearty breakfast of pancakes and eggs. After breakfast, my brother and I inflated the raft and paddled across the lake, catching several trout on the way. Mom made a doll for my sister out of a small log covered with a dishtowel with a face drawn on it. What a great place to be!

All too soon, the two weeks had passed, and it was time to return. The Millers had returned earlier. We packed the saddlebags, loaded the horses, and began our journey home. After we had ridden most of the day, my father announced, "We are lost."

> *We had neither map nor compass. We had not seen another human being other than our party the whole time we were camping.*

Those were frightening words. He admitted that we had lost the trail several hours ago and had been circling around for some time without finding the trail. We had neither map nor compass. We had not seen another human being other than our party the whole time we were camping, so it was not likely someone else would come to our rescue. Dad was silent as my brother asked, "What shall we do?"

Mother spoke next. "Let's pray and ask Jesus to help us." We all agreed that that was a good idea. As Mother prayed, Dad was impressed to let Mother's horse lead the way and give it free rein.

With Mother in the lead, allowing her horse to go wherever it wanted, we traveled on. As darkness descended, we arrived at a pack station where the ranger allowed us to stay for the night and then drove Dad to the trailhead where our truck was parked. God had answered our prayer.

The next problem was to get the horse trailer fixed. Dad was able to call from the pack station to a mechanic, who was willing to come up and repair the trailer. In the meantime, we had to search for the wheel. We systematically searched for over an hour without success. Finally, in desperation, Mother again suggested that we pray. And that we did, trusting that God knew where the wheel was. And sure enough. Mother was impressed to walk on up the road a few hundred feet, and there was the wheel. Soon the trailer was repaired, the horses loaded, and we were on our way home.

"I call on the Lord in my distress, and he answers me"
(Ps. 120:1).

2. The Making of a Missionary

My father and mother often gave board and room to literature evangelists, who we used to call colporteurs. I remember as a child sitting at their feet, listening to their stories of how they were able to share Christ with those whom they met during the day. That planted in my heart a desire to be a missionary. I was also very interested in medical work. I began to thrive on books about medical missionaries and their work.

When I was a senior at Monterey Bay Academy, a group of teachers came down from Pacific Union College to test us and encourage us to attend their college. After taking some tests, I sat down with one of the professors, who explained to me that I was not college material and that it would be better to go to a trade school. I felt betrayed and frustrated. Didn't God want me to be a medical missionary? I called my father, who had never had the chance to go to college. He asked me what I wanted to be, and I told him I wanted to be a medical missionary. He then said, "Go to college." I went.

Since I had written that I wanted to be a medical missionary on the entrance application, I was assigned to the chemistry professor. That meant that I would be a chemistry major as part of my pre-med course. Now, understand that I did not really like chemistry and felt that I was being set up for failure, so I went to the professor and told him how I felt. His reply was to go and see the biology professor. This was good news as I loved biology, especially marine biology.

The biology professor was very gracious and sat down with me to discuss my life's goals. I told him I wanted to be a medical missionary. Then he shocked me by saying, "Why don't you take physical therapy?" He explained to me that therapists can be missionaries and that as a therapist, I would have more time with a patient than a physician would; a time to share the Lord. If I started out with Pre-PT and then decided to take medicine, I could make that decision at several points in my education. I really liked that idea, and so changed my major to pre-physical therapy.

At the end of the first quarter, my grades were deplorable. I was failing. The academic dean called me to her office and told me that if my grades did not improve in the next quarter, I would have to leave college. Again, in discouragement, I called my dad. He again asked me what I wanted to do in life, and I told him I wanted to be a medical missionary. He advised me to reduce my class load and my workload and continue. I did, and my grades came up.

After the two years of pre-physical therapy, I applied to Loma Linda University's Physical Therapy program. I was accepted. During the two years at Pacific Union College, I met and fell in love with Jeanie Escobar. We planned on getting married just before beginning my course at Loma Linda University. That summer, I moved to San Bernardino to live with my aunt and uncle and to find work and a place to live after marriage. I was able to get a good job as an electrician.

During my time off that summer, I looked for a place where we could live. All the housing was filled with students. About that time, my grandmother came for a visit, and I asked her to look for an apartment for me. When I got home from work, she announced that she had bought a house for me for $5,000 and that I could pay her installments each month. Wow! It was an old house and needed a lot of TLC. And so I began fixing up the old house in my spare time. Unfortunately, it also took money for the repairs.

At the end of the summer, we were married and moved into our home. I need to explain that my father had told me that when I got married, I was on my own, and he would not pay for further education. So, now we are living in Loma Linda, all my money was spent on fixing up the old house, and there was no money for my tuition. I walked into the School of Physical Therapy dean's office to explain that I may have to stay out a year and work. He looked at me and said he had a full scholarship for me if I wanted it. Praise the Lord!!

"I will instruct you and teach you in the way you should go; I will counsel you and watch over you" (Ps. 32:8).

3. God's Math Is Different

After our marriage and my beginning of school, Jeanie was able to get a job in the Loma Linda Hospital business office. I also worked on Sundays. Our budget was very tight, which led to discussions on how much to give to the Lord's work. We both agreed that we would always put God first and our needs second. God blessed, and we were able to survive the first couple of years, thanks to God and the food baskets that occasionally would land on our doorstep.

> *We both agreed that we would always put God first and our needs second.*

Near the end of my second year of physical therapy training, Jeanie was assigned to a new boss who was extremely difficult to work with. Because it was causing her so much stress, she was advised to resign, which she did. Now our income would be very little until she was able to get another job. It was at this time that our faith was tested.

One Sunday evening, I sat down at my desk to pay some bills. I carefully added each bill to see if we had enough money to pay them. I compared the total with the balance in the checkbook. We would be short. I added the bills again and compared with the checkbook. There would not be enough money to pay all the bills. I discussed this with Jeanie and listed options. One option would be to pay the bills and pay our tithe later. Then, we remembered our promise to God that we would put Him first, so we prayed, reminding God of His promises. I returned to my desk, prioritized the bills, and began to write the checks. This first check was to the church for tithes and offerings. I then began to pay the bills. An amazing thing happened. After paying the tithe/offerings AND ALL the bills, there was still some money in the bank! Following this experience, we have always paid our tithe and offerings first. As a result, God has blessed us abundantly, and we have never been short financially.

> **"Know therefore that the LORD your God is God; he is the faithful God, keeping his covenant of love to a thousand generations of those who love him and keep his commands" (Deut. 7:9).**

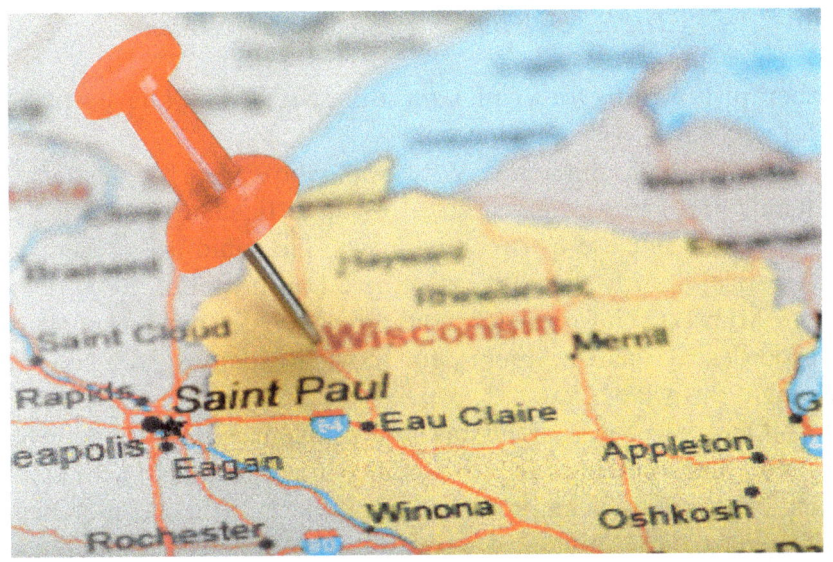

4. Another Disappointment

During the final days of my physical therapy training, a representative for the General Conference of Seventh-day Adventists came and gave a chapel talk. He talked about missions and the need for workers in the mission field. He stated that whatever your medical occupation was, you were needed. Here was our opportunity to sign up for mission service.

I met with the rep after the chapel and was given a stack of papers to fill out. Jeanie and I worked our way through the pages, filling out the blanks as best we knew how. Then, with a prayer of commitment, I returned the papers and had an interview. When I told him that I would be graduating from physical therapy school and that we were committed to mission service, he leaned back in his chair and said, "You know, we don't have a lot of calls for physical therapists. In fact, I have several therapists waiting for a call. I am sorry, but we don't have a place for you now."

I was so disappointed. What was God's plan for our lives? Jeanie and I prayed much about this and finally decided that if God could not use us overseas, maybe He could use us here in America. Shortly thereafter, I received an invitation to work in the Midwest. Unfortunately, the employer did not pay moving expenses. We had no money for moving expenses, so again we sought the will of God.

One day, I was discussing this problem with a friend. She stated that sometimes the local conference would help with moving expenses to bring professional people into their conference. The next day, Monday, I wrote to the Wisconsin Conference and asked if there might be some funds to help us move. **That Thursday** I received a response! (Remember snail mail?) The conference would pay for our moving expenses if we stayed in that conference for at least five years. This was another indication that God was leading.

We moved to Green Bay, Wisconsin, and began our work. After we were settled, the pastor, Elder Elmer Rasmussen, met me at the door of the church on Sabbath and asked if I would be willing to preach. I hesitated. I didn't think that being a medical missionary, I would have to preach. I finally agreed. He scheduled me to speak several months later. The time flew by, and soon I was face to face with a first-time preaching appointment. I was scared and nervous. I studied and prayed. I wrote and rewrote the sermon. During the last week, Jeanie told me that I was driving her crazy with my nervousness. Sabbath morning, I rose early and walked down along the river close to our apartment. I told God that I could not do this and to provide someone else to preach that Sabbath. No answer came.

Then it was time. I came to the pulpit and announced my opening text. It was a tongue-twister, and I fumbled. The audience was obviously nervous for me. Finally, I told the audience to read the text themselves, and I would go on with the sermon. I kept praying for the Holy Spirit to take over. Suddenly, I was speaking freely, and there was a hush over the audience. Soon,

I noticed that tears were flowing on some faces. God's message came through, and I don't even remember all that I said! Praise God for Holy Spirit power!

> **"I will pour out my spirit on you. I will make my words known to you" (Prov. 1:23, NLV).**

5. The Call of Uncle Sam

It was 1966. Jeanie and I decided to attend the General Conference session of the Seventh-day Adventist Church for the last weekend. We were anxious to see Jeanie's parents, who were delegates. When we arrived, we were very surprised when friends came up to us and said that we had been voted by the General Conference to send us to Brazil as missionaries. Our dreams were being fulfilled.

Over the next few weeks, we packed, sold our belongings, and made plans to go to Brazil. But God had other plans. Two weeks before our sailing date, I was drafted into the U.S. Army. What a disappointment! I was assigned to Fort Sam Huston, Texas, where I would go through basic training. Even though we were very disappointed, I did have the opportunity to share Jesus with other men in the barracks. Some were raised Christian but were using this opportunity away from parents to live the wild life. I prayed with these men, and some turned to the Lord.

It was at the height of the Vietnam war. I desired to use my profession as a physical therapist while in the military but was told by my sergeant that I would be going to Vietnam as a medic. I was not convinced. The sergeant was a very opinionated person and was not going to be told anything. I asked to go up to the personnel office to see if I could use my PT training in the military. He refused to let me go. It was very demoting to have been a professional in the community and now be a buck private and have to be told everything to do or not to do.

Toward the end of basic training, I was returning from the chapel on Sabbath and spotted a sign directing to the physical therapy department. I made a mental note and headed back to my company area. Later that week, the sergeant marched us to the quartermaster building to get an item of clothing that we would need. As we neared the building, the sergeant told us to go into the building and be back in thirty minutes while he waited under the shade of a lone tree. It was a hot day. All the windows and doors of the building were open. I walked into the building, went straight out the back door, and ran up to the physical therapy office. I was now AWOL (absent without leave) from my company area.

> *I was now AWOL (absent without leave) from my company area.*

I walked into the director's office, where I met a very lovely lady of high rank. I told her of my plight, and she responded, "I need you right now. We are short of physical therapists." I was elated. She called in people from the personnel office who began the work of getting me assigned to the hospital after basic training and also to start the process of getting me a commission of second lieutenant. When the interview was over, I told her that I was AWOL from my company area and would be in trouble when I went back. She looked over to a lieutenant and asked if he would drive me to my company area. When we arrived, the sergeant met us, saluted the lieutenant, and said to me, "Private Putz, anytime you want to go to the personnel office or the hospital, let me know, and I will give you a jeep and a driver."

When we finished basic training, the men received their orders to go on to AIT (Advanced Individual Training). My orders were to go to truck-driving school at Camp Bullis instead of the hospital. When I arrived, I called back to the personnel office to find out why I wasn't assigned to the hospital. They told me that there was some mix-up but to finish that school and then to report to their office. Driving the troops around on the base was part of the training, so I drove for a few weeks; then, it was time to head home for the Christmas break.

I was so anxious to see my wife and be home again, but there was a problem. We were told that due to the high number of troops in training, that there was not enough housing in the community, and that we were forbidden to bring back our car or wife. As we moved through the checkout line, they gave us a small piece of paper on which we were to sign saying that we promised not to bring back our wives or our cars. There was no time to go to personnel, so I prayed that I would not have to sign since I would be assigned to the hospital, and I wanted my wife to live with me, and I would need the car. I slipped the unsigned paper into my pocket and moved forward in the line. Suddenly, just when the sergeant asked for my paper, a general walked in. The sergeant shouted, "Attention!" in a loud, booming voice. It is rare that any high-ranking officer would ever walk through the barracks, and the sergeant was obviously shook up. After the general had walked out the other door, the sergeant turned to me and said, "Sign out and go." I did, with the paper still in my pocket unsigned. Can angels be generals?

After the break, my wife and I returned to the base to try to find housing. There was none. At every apartment there were a few soldiers and wives waiting to see if there was any opening. Friday came, and no place to live. I had to check in on Monday. Friday evening came, and no apartment or place to live. I cried. I would have to send my wife back home on Sunday. As the Sabbath drew on, we prayed for help. Should we continue to look on Sabbath or attend church? We decided to go to the church service in town.

It was communion Sabbath, and during the foot-washing ceremony, a lady approached my wife and acknowledged they had met before. It was at the San Bernardino Church in California. They took part together, and then the lady asked us home for dinner. That was such a blessing!! When we told her about our problem, she said that her neighbor had rentals and would ask her after sundown. She did call the neighbor. The lady had prepared one apartment for another couple who were coming later, but she said that she could give them another apartment, and we could have that one. God tries us and then blesses us.

We moved into our new apartment on Sunday, and I reported to the post early Monday morning. The new sergeant was very nice and allowed me to go up to the personnel office. The problem was that I was on a new order, assigning me to the hospital, but that I was not taken off of the old troop list. The office gave me a stack of new orders, and I headed to the hospital, thankful that the Lord was in charge.

It took several months before my commission came through. In the meantime, I worked as a therapist but was still a private. One morning at 10:00 a.m., the lieutenant colonel came to me and told me I had to be at General Black's office by noon to receive my commission. I rushed home to change into my dress uniform, after which I was to clear the AMEDS Company before reporting but not to check out. Clearing the company meant that one had to go to all the post services like the golf club, the officers' club, etc., and get a signature that I didn't owe any money. There was a long list of services to go to. The sergeant at AMEDS Company was not helpful when I asked if I could use the telephone to call the various services to get their initials. He told me to get out and "hoof it." Fortunately, I had my friend's car (we did ride-sharing) and was able to get it done and be at the general's office by noon.

I was commissioned as a second lieutenant, and then received my bar and officer's clothing. I was elated! Now I had to return to AMEDS Company and sign out. As I walked in the door, the sergeant's mouth dropped open, and he just stared at me. Finally, he spoke in a faltering voice, "Weren't ... you ... the ... one ... who ... was ... in ... here this morning ... to sign out?"

"Yes," I replied, "and you were not very respectful to me, were you?"

"No," he replied.

My next words shocked me. "Get down and give me 100 pushups." Down on the floor he went, counting as he pushed up. After about twenty pushups, I told him that was enough. He stood up, and I said to him, "Sergeant, I want you to learn to respect all people no matter what rank or ethnicity."

"Yes, sir!" he replied, and I went on my way after signing out.

After receiving my appointment as a second lieutenant, I was assigned to the hospital at Fort Leonard Wood in Missouri. The first six months were wonderful. Then the major, my boss, was transferred out, and a new major came. This new major was very upset that she had to be assigned to Fort Leonard Wood and not San Francisco or Hawaii. You see, Fort Leonard Wood was often called "Little Korea." She had just returned from Korea. She took out her frustration on all of the staff. One day, she announced that I would be expected to work every other Saturday. I explained to her that I was willing to help in an emergency and come in on Sundays but was not willing to do regular work on Saturday, as it was my Sabbath. She wasn't happy about that. After another week, she ordered me to work on the next Saturday. At that point I went to her supervisor, a light colonel, and told him my problem. He suggested that I bring my Bible to work and let the non-professional helpers do the routine work. And so I did. That was not the answer. I was constantly having a barrage of questions and telephone calls. It was not a worshipful Sabbath. The next Monday, when I arrived, the helpers were crying, and when asked why, they told me that the major had threatened them with punishment if they worked for me again. Two weeks later, I was again ordered to work on Saturday, and if I refused, I would be court-martialed. I refused.

Nothing was said after that. I was harassed by her, and she made my work very difficult. What I didn't know at that time was that she was keeping a record of all my faults and mistakes in order to block my promotion. She wrote an eight-page report as to why I shouldn't be promoted. She sent the papers to be signed by the next in command, Dr. Virchel Wood, an orthopedic surgeon. He was an Adventist and a good friend of mine. He refused to sign. Next, she took it to the chief of staff. He saw through her plight and refused to sign. Then she took it to the commanding officer of the hospital. He refused to sign it. He had worked at the Adventist Hospital in Boulder, Colorado, so knew what Adventists believed. Following her inability to get a signature, she took a leave of absence and went to Washington, DC, and the Pentagon to get them to support her. They didn't. They transferred her to a small hospital where she could receive counseling. It is amazing how God put all the right people in the right places to vindicate me and the Sabbath. I was promoted to first lieutenant and assigned to Fort Eustis Hospital in Virginia as chief therapist. Following my tour of military service, we returned to Wisconsin to fulfill my pledge to the conference. If we are faithful, God will provide for us.

"Do what is right and good in the LORD**'s sight, so that it may go well with you" (Deut. 6:18).**

6. Another Test of Faith

After leaving the army, I took a partner position in southwest Wisconsin and served a couple of nursing homes and one hospital. After a couple of years, the partnership went sour. It was obvious that to succeed we would have to move to a new area. I gave my three months' notice and began to send out résumés. No replies. My partner and I had just begun to negotiate a contract with a nursing home in Rhinelander, Wisconsin, so I asked if he would be willing to let me take that contract. He agreed.

We drove up to Rhinelander, about four hours north, and talked to the administrator of the nursing home. After the interview, Jeanie looked at me and asked how I felt about the job. I replied that I did not feel good about it. She felt the same. Now what? What was God's plan? We prayed and then decided to go home via the conference office in Madison to learn which towns in Wisconsin had church schools so our daughter could have a Christian education. We specifically wanted to meet with the conference president, Elder Mittleider.

As we entered the freeway, the traffic was very heavy. As we moved along slowly, Jeanie said, "Look out your side window." I looked, and right beside us was Elder Mittleider and his wife. I honked and waved and motioned for them to pull off at the wayside that came at that very moment. We explained to the Mittleiders our dilemma. He said that he had just come from the Oconto area, where they were starting a new school and that the four-church district was poor, and they needed professional members to help. He also gave us a list of all the church schools in Wisconsin.

The next day, I called the Oconto hospital to see if there was a need for a physical therapist. The administrator explained that they had an excellent PT and that he also served several of the nursing homes in the area. He felt that there was not a need for another PT. I then called all the other facilities in the towns where there was a church school. All answers were the same: no openings. Now what? "Lord, please help us to find the right job where we can serve You the best," was our prayer. Two months went by. Nothing. Jeanie was feeling very insecure and anxious. We continued to pray and sent out more résumés.

Just before my three-month notice of quitting was up, I received a call from the administrator of the Oconto hospital. He explained that a few minutes after my initial call, his PT came in and gave his resignation. He was sorry that it took so long to inform me. I met with the administrator the next day and discussed a contract. I made the first offer, and he countered with a better offer, which I accepted.

God had tried us again and, at the last moment, answered our prayers.

God had tried us again and, at the last moment, answered our prayers. We packed our things and moved. When we arrived, we found that there was little available housing that fit our needs. The first Sabbath, we were welcomed by a lovely older couple at church who invited us to dinner. They were so gracious and allowed us to stay with them until we could find housing! After two weeks of rainy weather, we had not found a home. We kept praying. It was decided to look at a small town a few miles to the west. As we drove into Oconto Falls, suddenly, the sun came out as if God was saying, "This is the place." Within minutes, we found a lovely home in a wooded neighborhood that was just right for us. We were able to get a VA loan, and so the purchase was made.

After a couple of weeks, the pastor of the district and the conference evangelist came to visit. They strongly encouraged us to join the church a few miles away. We hesitated because we wanted to check out the other churches in the district. They wanted us to go to the annual business meeting. I finally gave in and went to the meeting in which they chose their officers and made other decisions. Their attending membership was about thirty. The head elder and only elder had been in position for more than fifty years. The Sabbath school superintendent had been in office for more than thirty years. The church had only one service a week and had no children's divisions or anything for the youth. There was one young family our age. It was obvious that they needed help. Someone suggested that I take the head eldership subject to our membership transfer. Not wanting to hurt the aged head elder, I refused. I finally gave in to be a second elder. Was this because God wanted us to live west of my work and be closer to this church?

After our membership was changed, I went to visit the old elder. He was a godly man in his seventies or eighties. He, as well as most members, were farmers. I helped him chop wood as we talked about the church. I asked if they had prayer meeting, to which he responded that they tried it some thirty years ago, and no one came.

The next week I visited him again, and while pitching hay asked if we might try again to have a mid-week service. "It won't work," he said. "We are farmers; we don't have time to go to church in the middle of the week." Again, the next week, I asked him if I could try and start a mid-week service. He repeated again that it wouldn't work but that I could try if I wanted to, but he would not be able to attend.

Another Test of Faith

At that time, the Adventist churches in America were putting on a program called Testimony Countdown. It was a nine-week program to go through Ellen White's nine volumes of the *Testimonies for the Church*. The material was written for both children and adults. Jeanie and I decided to use that material. I went to the conference office and purchased the study guides, leadership guides, and ten sets of the Testimonies for the Church. We then visited each family in their homes. These church members informed us that they would like to do this program, but they did not have any of E. G. White's books. I told them that they were on sale and that I had an extra set in my car I could sell them. They purchased the books.

What a surprise we had when at the first meeting, every member attended. We were all blessed, and they all came, including the old elder, each night throughout the program. Praise the Lord for what the Holy Spirit did during those meetings. The mid-week services continued, and my wife and the other young mother were able to get the children's Sabbath School going. I began to train other members on how to get more involved. This is where God wanted us!

> **"In his heart a man plans his course, but the Lord determines his steps" (Prov. 16:9).**

7. The Angel and the Boat

It was a beautiful fall day in Wisconsin. The leaves were turning to their bright yellow and orange colors. Some friends, Paul and Ethel, had called and wanted to go sailing on Lake Michigan. My boat was just a small thirteen-foot sailboat. As we backed the boat down into the water, we noticed that the wind was beginning to pick up. We were not alarmed because the more wind, the better for a sailboat. With the mast up and the sails flapping in the wind, we headed out, just the other couple and me. Everything was perfect for a great day on the water.

We limited our course to tacking back and forth in the sheltered area of a small bay. Then, it happened. A rogue wave washed over the side of the boat, causing it to sink deeper into the water. Then, since the side of the boat was so low, the waves kept pouring in. We kept trying to bail the water but to no avail. The boat went

The Angel and the Boat

vertical. It had flotation chambers in the bow, so the boat floated vertically. We had life preservers on, so felt fairly safe. The idea was to swim, pushing the boat toward land and hope to reach land before we passed the point of the peninsula. We swam and swam, pushing the boat closer to the shore. Unfortunately, the wind was pushing us out toward the middle of Lake Michigan.

My wife was watching helplessly on the shore. Some young people on shore were also watching, and they called the coast guard, who refused to help. One of the young people decided to swim out to help us, not realizing that he would only contribute to the problem. When he was about halfway out, he began to go down. He was yelling for help, but no one was close enough to help him.

We were being blown out into the open sea, missing the point. We prayed. Just after we prayed, we heard the putt-putt of a small fishing boat. We looked up to see a man with a wide-brimmed hat heading our way. He stopped and picked up the drowning kid and then headed toward us. He threw me a line and told me not to touch his boat, but hold on to the line with one hand and onto my boat with the other hand. He also said that when my feet touched the ground, to let the line go. And so we started toward land.

Soon, my feet touched the bottom as we neared the shore. I let the line go, pulled the boat in as far as I could, and helped Ethel onto the shore. I then turned to thank the man, but there was no man and no boat. We could see miles up and down the shore—no man and no boat. Was it an angel? I think so. Can angels make boats and motors?

"The salvation of the righteous comes from the LORD; he is their stronghold in time of trouble" (Ps. 37:39).

8. Carol and the Truancy

Our first child, Carol, was five years old. She was a very bright girl, full of personality. We were living in a nice neighborhood in Oconto Falls, Wisconsin. Now let's go back five years. We were unable to have children, so we decided to adopt a child. We had applied to several agencies without success. We began praying earnestly for a child. There was an eighteen-year-old girl in Colorado who had gotten pregnant and was thrown out of the home. She moved to California with some friends.

Prior to her delivery, she told the doctor that she wanted to give her baby up for adoption. Since she did not know anyone who would take her baby, the doctor's nurse was given the responsibility to find a family to adopt the child. She put the word out and began to receive many calls. Unable to decide which family should receive the child, she made it a matter of prayer. Jeanie's mother

Carol and the Truancy

heard about this and called. When the nurse received the call, she had just told the Lord that she would give the baby to the next person who called. My mother-in-law called us and said that we had a baby. A few weeks later, we drove to California to claim our precious child. She was only three days old. We named her Carol Jean.

We headed to Wisconsin, where I would be working. Evidently, the California hospital sent word to the state of Wisconsin that we would be moving there. Shortly after we arrived, we received notice from the state that it was illegal to bring a child into that state for the purpose of adoption and that the social services were going to pick up the baby and place her in a foster home. We panicked and immediately began to pray. We lived in a very small town. Where could we find a competent lawyer to help us? A friend referred us to an attorney. Fortunately, he was a very sharp attorney. He immediately worked with the judge to get us licensed as a foster home and then placed our own child into our home while the adoption proceedings were taking place.

> *When the nurse received the call, she had just told the Lord that she would give the baby to the next person who called.*

Now, fast forward. One of our neighbors notified the local public school's truancy department that we had not put Carol in school at the age of five. State law mandated that all children must be enrolled by this age. The truancy officer called and insisted that we put her in school. This gave us some trepidation that the social services would get involved again, so we again took it to God in prayer. A few days later, there was a knock on the door, and the man wanted to know if we were willing to sell our home. I had purchased a piece of property in the country from a friend after I had done some electrical work for him. The notice of the sale was put in the legal section of the local newspaper. I told him that I planned to build there sometime in the future when we had the money. He offered a good price and said he would buy our home and give us six months to build. The sale went through, and we built our dream home in the country. We never heard from the truancy department again. God is good!

"O Lord, you are my God; I will exalt you and praise your name, for in perfect faithfulness you have done marvelous things, things planned long ago" (Isa. 25:1).

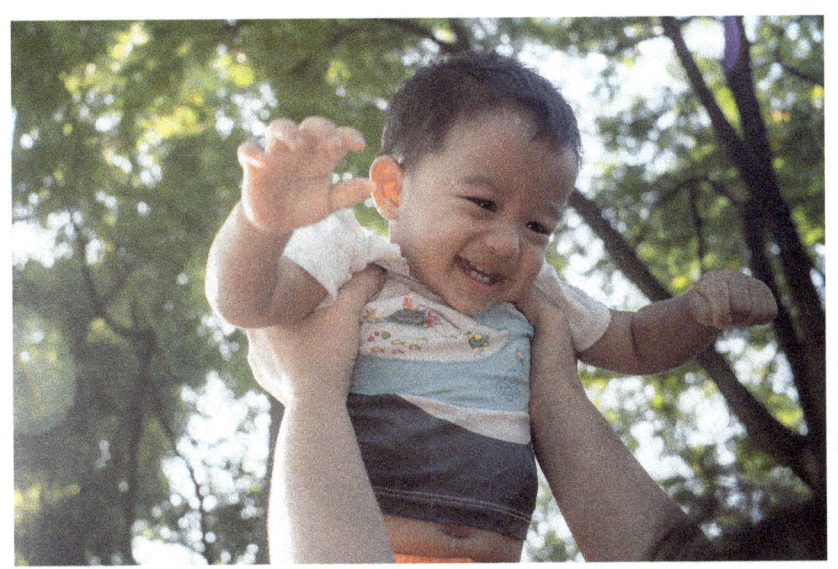

9. Another Miracle Baby

After the adoption of Carol was complete, we were told by the social services that we should not do another private adoption, but to contact them, and they would have a child for us. When Carol was three years old, we applied to the state for another baby. Months went by and no baby. We began to look in other places without success.

Our file had been placed in the Northern Wisconsin district. The state rearranged the districts, which put our file with the southern district. That district included Green Bay, Milwaukee, and Madison, the three most populous cities. We were notified that it might take eight years for us to receive a baby. Again, this called for prayer.

We flew out to California to visit parents and also to explore the possibility of finding another baby. When we returned, there was a message on our phone, asking us to call the Social Service Office. We called, and they explained that somehow our file had not been transferred to the southern district by mistake. A child had just come up for adoption, and the social worker felt that he was a match for us. She called the southern district and told them that our file was not moved and asked if they could go ahead and place the baby in our home. They approved, and so we received little Stuart Dale at age six months. Another miracle!

When Stuart was about three, there was a good accumulation of snow at our home. One late Sunday morning, we decided that we would take the kids sledding. We walked out through our backwoods until we found a nice sloped hill without any trees in the path for a sled run. As we walked up the hill, Stuart, in his excitement, ran ahead and placed his sled on the top of the back side of the hill. The sled flew backward down the back side headed toward a barbed wire fence. We frantically yelled for him to fall over, but he kept going faster and faster. Spontaneously our prayers flew up to God. Suddenly, just before going under the wire at neck level, the sled hit a buried log, and the sled flew over the wire without even touching Stuart! God must have placed that log there years ago for that purpose. We praised God for His protection.

> **"Sons are a heritage from the LORD, children a reward from him" (Ps. 127:3).**

10. Japan

We awoke with a start as the telephone was loudly ringing. It was 1976. The caller identified himself as Elder Johnson from the headquarters of the Seventh-day Adventist Church. He was extending a call to us to go as missionaries to Japan. This called for a decision that we were not prepared to make. We felt that God had called us to Wisconsin. My practice was growing, and we were actively involved in the local church, including giving Bible studies to non-members. We had also just built a new home in the country, which was a blessing from the Lord. What was God's will? We felt like Nehemiah when he said, "We are doing a great work here" (see Neh. 6:3).

We told Elder Johnson that we would pray about it, but felt that God wanted us where we were. He called again the next week. We told him no. He called again the next week, and I told him that

I struggled with learning a new language. He informed me that most of the employees in the Tokyo hospital spoke English. (Not true, as we learned later). A couple of months later, as I was walking through the kitchen, my wife startled me by saying, "Are you sure that it is God's will that we stay here and not go to Japan?"

After a moment of speechlessness, I responded by saying that I would go downstairs to my office and ask God again what He wanted. I got on my knees in the middle of the office and told the Lord that, if it was His will, we were willing to go to Japan, but that we needed Him to tell us. At that moment, I heard a voice in my head that said GO. I said, "I think I hear You saying go, and if that is so, please give me a sign. Have the conference call me again today." Thirty minutes later, Elder Johnson called again, saying that he felt impressed to call us one more time. So, after selling our home we were off to Japan.

> *At that moment, I heard a voice in my head that said GO.*

"Whether you turn to the right or to the left, your ears will hear a voice behind you, saying, 'This is the way; walk in it'" (Isa. 30:21).

11. His Hands Are My Hands and My Hands Are His Hands

We arrived in Japan without knowing a word in Japanese. One of my subordinates could speak a little, I mean little, English. In order to treat effectively, a practitioner must first get a concise history and be able to understand what the main symptoms are. I was not able to get any of that information without a good interpreter, so after discussing the matter with the administrator, I was allowed to attend a language school for half a day. That meant that when other students were studying for the next day's assignment, I had to work. Progress was slow. Carol went off to elementary school and picked up the language very fast. I was jealous. After learning some basics, I still didn't know how to understand my patients, so I was sent to a second school. That was no help. Finally a retired nurse, Miss Takagi, came to my rescue. She was fluent in English and, of course, Japanese. She would stay with me and interpret while I asked questions and gave instructions. She then would drill me on how to say the most common sentences that I used and that the patients would respond with. After about two years of her tutorial help, I was able to work alone without her. That was a gift from God.

After living in Japan for about one year, the hospital decided to conduct a free clinic in Sapporo, the northernmost island. I was asked to accompany the medical team. We were very limited in what we could take, as dental chairs and equipment were absolutely the most important to take. I was able to take a folding treatment table, a few sheets, and a pillow. I could not take any other physical therapy equipment and wondered what I would be able to do. I prayed that God would use my hands.

When we arrived, the building was full of people needing medical treatment. We set up our stations and began seeing patients. I must have seen at least fifty patients that day, and all of them were helped. Through the assigned interpreter we had prayer with each patient. God worked many miracles that day in my section with only my hands.

> "How blessed is he who considers the helpless; The LORD will deliver him in a day of trouble. The LORD will protect him, and keep him alive, And he shall be called blessed upon the earth" (Ps. 41:1–2, NASB).

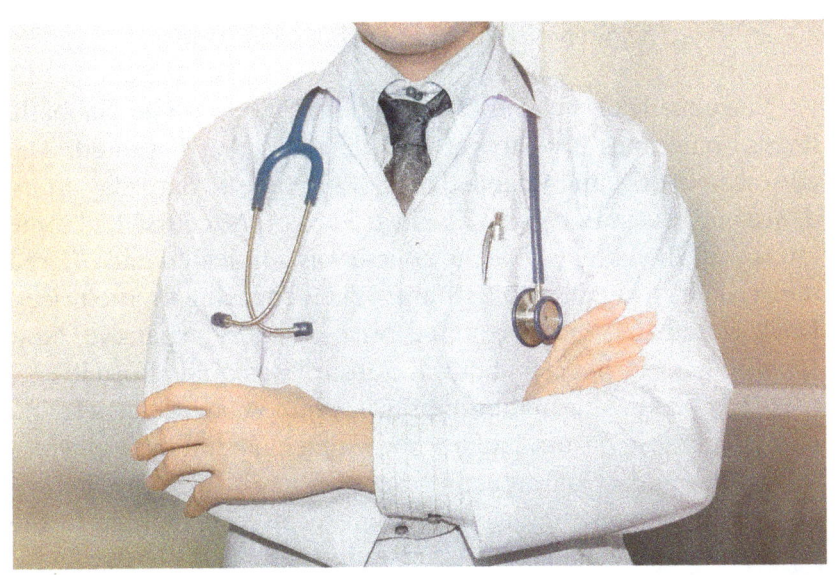

12. Medical School?

It is always frustrating when one is not able to do what one is trained to do. For example, when the army sergeant would not allow me to explore how I could use my profession as a physical therapist. The same frustration occurred in my practice. After I had been out of school for several years, I began to realize that many of my patients were not improving as I had hoped. I tried very hard to follow the orders of the physicians and apply the treatments correctly, but I felt that the success rate was not there. One day I discussed this with a colleague. He suggested that I take some advanced training. One class that he recommended was going to be held in Las Vegas, Nevada. It was a class in orthopedic physical therapy. I attended the two-week course and was excited with what I learned.

Since many of the courses being offered were on the Sabbath, it was sometimes hard to get into the class that I wanted. The advanced course that I needed next didn't require Saturday attendance and was in Bermuda. The instructor of the course had some interest in the hotel where the course was conducted and offered the students a significant discount. When checking on the prices, I discovered that the discounted price was very expensive. Now what? I needed that class but was not sure we could afford it.

After making it a matter of prayer, I remembered that a friend of my parents, a pastor, had been working in Bermuda, so I wrote to the Bermuda Conference of Seventh-day Adventists, hoping he would recognize my name. I soon received a reply from the president of the conference, saying that they had a guest house on the beach that we could use for a hundred dollars for the full two weeks! They even supplied me with a moped to get to my classes. What a blessing. Taking our two children, Carol, age five, and Stuart, age three, we headed to Bermuda. While I attended the classes, the family enjoyed the beach. The family friend, who was a local pastor, greeted us warmly, and we spent some wonderful times together.

I continued to take further classes in orthopedics, many of them for physicians and therapists. My practice was now becoming very rewarding and successful; however, that brought on some frustration, since what treatment the physicians were ordering did not always agree with what I had learned. Some of the docs were willing to try some new things, but others were not.

Now, while working in Japan, the physicians were suggesting that I go back to medical school in order to do what I was trained to do. They suggested that I apply to medical schools in the Philippines. The tuition there was much less than in America, so I applied and was accepted into two schools. Since we had sold our home before going to Japan, we had enough money to attend all five years. Was this in God's plan?

My wife and I flew to the Philippines to decide which school to attend and to pay the entrance fees. We were treated royally by the Adventists there. We were given nice guest rooms, and they offered to take us around to the various tourist sites. It was

Medical School? 41

a very memorable trip. I decided that the school in Cebu City was probably the best. When we flew into the island where the school was located, the conference president picked us up and gave us a guest room. The deadline to pay the entrance fee was 5:00 p.m. on Friday. That day we did some last-minute shopping before starting for the school to pay. Just before leaving the guest room, I noticed that our flight tickets were missing. We searched all through our luggage. We went back to some of the stores where we had purchased items, but no tickets. Now panic set in, as the tickets were not refundable, and we had to leave on Sunday. Again, we prayed. We decided to go to the local airline ticket office down the street to see if they would give us duplicate tickets. The conference president said we should not walk, but that he would take us. When getting into the car, I noticed something familiar above the back seat. It was our tickets! I had evidentially dropped them when riding from the airport, and his wife, not realizing what they were, threw them back when she used the car later. I glanced down at my watch. It was now 5:40. We had missed the deadline.

As we flew home that Sunday, we tried to understand what God's plan was. While in the Philippines, the medical students were telling me what a great school this was and encouraging me to come, while the wives of the students were telling my wife not to come because of the dangers to foreigners and, especially, children. After much thought and prayer, we felt that God had another plan.

> *After much thought and prayer, we felt that God had another plan.*

Since we had advised the Tokyo hospital that we would be going to medical school, they had called another therapy couple to take our place. Now in a few weeks, I would be finished in Japan, and where were we to go? We prayed for guidance. No answer came. We left Japan and flew to Hawaii, where Jeanie's father was serving as a pastor. While there, I explored other medical schools. None of them seemed to be where God wanted us.

Leaving Jeanie and the kids, I flew to California to spend a few days with my father. He had just returned from Weimar Institute, where he had gone through the twenty-one-day lifestyle enhancement program. He was very excited about it and insisted that I go up there and visit it. I resisted the idea, but he insisted. On arrival, I was met by Dick Winn, the director and an old classmate. He stated that he was happy that God had brought me to Weimar, as they were in need of a physical therapist. I was not sure. We stayed several days, and as I observed how those very sick patients were improving while undergoing the natural treatments, God began to work on my heart. This seemed to be where God wanted me. I called Jeanie and shared this with her. She was not convinced. I prayed that if it was God's will that we go there, that He would convince her. She balked.

Later, I convinced her to come and check it out. We stayed there for several weeks. She kept saying she did not want to come and live with these very conservative people and wear long dresses, etc. She cried every night, saying that she knew I felt God was calling us there, but that she did not feel that way. I continued to pray.

Finally, one day, she said to me. "If we could put a mobile home up away from the center of the campus, I would be willing to come."

I rejoiced, and we headed to Sacramento to search for the right home. She found one. Several weeks later, we moved in, and we spent three-and-one-half wonderful years at Weimar Institute. It was a delightful time, and the children did well in the school. But the most important thing that we learned was how to apply healthful treatments and teach others how to change their lifestyles to enhance their physical health as well as their spiritual health. This was where God wanted us at that time.

"I will instruct you and teach you in the way you should go; I will counsel you and watch over you" (Ps. 32:8).

13. The Hawaiian Health Center

After spending more than three years at Weimar, we felt it was time for a break and took a vacation to Hawaii. Our longtime friends, Bob and Danetta Frost, were living there. Bob was serving as the treasurer of the Hawaiian conference. After making contact with them, Bob told us that the conference was interested in starting a health center similar to the one at Weimar Institute and asked if we would be willing to sit with the committee to determine where this should be located. We agreed. After several meetings, they asked us to travel to the different islands and make a recommendation as to where to locate the center.

We enjoyed visiting the different islands and basking in the sun. We visited Kahili Mountain Park on the northern flower island,

Kauai. This was a lovely spot where the local churches had started a twelve-grade school on leased land. (Very little land was sold at that time, so most businesses were granted long term leases.) The property had small cabins that could be used for staff housing or rented out. The property was located up close to the mountains yet not far from the beach. The flowers and flora were gorgeous. The air was clean, being away from any city. This seemed an ideal setting. The students of the school could work in the health center to help with their tuition, and the staff of the health center could teach some health classes at the school. There was plenty of room for gardens for the students and patients to work in.

We gave our report to the conference. They then asked us if we would be willing to come to Hawaii to run the program. We were elated. When we asked about the funding of the center, the conference president told us he didn't think it would be a problem to raise the money. On the flight back to California, we began to formulate plans for the center. I worked on the philosophy, staffing, finances, etc., while Jeanie began to sketch out the buildings and treatment rooms. When we returned to work at Weimar Institute, we turned in our notice that we would be moving to Hawaii.

As time moved on, the conference was not able to raise the necessary funds, and our replacements were arriving soon. Now what was God's plan this time? Should we proceed, trusting that God would provide the funds? Or was that presumption? We prayed earnestly to know God's will, but no answer came. Our hearts were set on Hawaii, but maybe God had a different plan.

Finally, I was offered an opportunity to go back into private practice in central California. We went to check it out and prayed that if it was God's will that we go there, He would show us a home in the country without us having to look for a long time. When we arrived, I purchased a newspaper and began searching the ads. One house stood out; an older home in the country.

As we drove by it, Jeanie said "I am not interested in that old place."

I was discouraged because I thought it looked great. We drove down the country road, and as we approached a golf course, Jeanie saw a street with newer homes. We turned. It was a short street with a cul-de-sac. There was one house for sale. I went to the door and was invited in. I motioned for Jeanie to follow. We fell in love with the house right away. It had a beautiful yard in which was a nice swimming pool, a fern garden, and decking. We were told that it had had an offer but that there was a stipulation that if the prospective buyers could not get their loan within a certain time, someone could outbid them. I offered a hundred dollars more and closed the deal. Now we felt more confidence that this was God's plan. We were very disappointed that the Hawaii Health Center never materialized.

I set up my practice, and the Lord blessed. There was an active church and church school for the kids. We started health classes for our patients which brought us fifteen to thirty people every month.

When I graduated from Loma Linda University School of Physical Therapy, I promised the Lord that I would pray with my patients and share Jesus with them. This was a rewarding experience as it led to many Bible studies and conversions. One such case stands out in my mind. Her name was Linda. Linda came into my office with neck pain resulting from a rear-end collision.

As she was escorted to the treatment room, she exclaimed, "I don't have time for this. I don't know why I had to come here."

I did the evaluation and began the treatment. I prayed for her when the treatment was finished, and she left. The next time she came in, as I started the treatment, I began to share Jesus with her by asking some simple questions.

She turned to me and with a loud, firm voice retorted, "Stop, I have had religion up to here (with her hand swiping across her forehead). Don't talk to me about it."

I was taken back and apologized. One of my PT aides just happened to be in the treatment room, putting some towels away. She was a new hire, a sweet and caring Catholic girl. She heard what I had said to Linda and started asking me questions about the gospel. Linda listened but could not say anything, since I was not talking to her.

At the next treatment session, the same aide was in the room again with Linda. This was very unusual for her to be cleaning or putting laundry away while a patient was in the room. Again, my aide took up the previous day's conversation and asked more questions about the gospel. Linda sat quietly without saying a word as I continued to share the good news of our salvation through Jesus.

At the end of the next treatment session, Linda turned to me and said, "I know why I had to come here." I asked her why? She said, "Because I needed to hear what you were saying to the aide."

I responded, "Are you ready to receive Jesus into your heart?"

She hesitated and said that she had something she had to do before she was ready. The next day as I worked with her, there was no conversation other than how her neck was feeling. At the end of the session, she turned to me and said, "I am ready." I invited her to pray right then and accept Jesus into her heart. She did. Over the next several months, we studied the Bible together. Soon, she was baptized into the church.

There is nothing more thrilling than to work with the Holy Spirit for the salvation of people.

"Whoever drinks the water I give him will never thirst. Indeed, the water I give him will become in him a spring of water welling up to eternal life" (John 4:14).

14. A Church Plant

One Thursday evening, a fellow member of our church called and said he was visiting with a pastor of the Spanish church in a nearby town. The member asked me to go to his home and meet this pastor. As we visited in the member's home, the pastor said he was concerned because the town we lived in did not have a work for Latinos. He informed us that there were more than 5,000 Latinos in our town, and there should be a work for them. There was a Latino Bible worker who was willing to come, but we would need to raise about $30,000 for his support for a year. We had a nice session of prayer and separated.

I was impressed that this was something that God wanted, so after arriving home, I began calling friends, family, and others of means, asking for pledges. Now, I am not a fundraiser, but I knew that the Holy Spirit would provide. By Sunday evening, the full $30,000 was pledged! What a miracle.

After the Bible worker had been working in the area for about six weeks, he called and said that he had fifty Bible studies going and needed a church to start services in. I began calling all the Sunday churches to see if they would rent to us. No one would. Again, this called for prayer. After about a week of driving through the poor side of town, I spotted a rundown Baptist church. I was able to find the pastor. He informed me that his membership had dropped to two or three members and that they could not keep the church building in repair. He was happy to rent to us if we promised, as part of the payment, to repair the church.

After the needed repairs were made, we started our services. It was decided that we should have a Spanish service at 8:00 a.m., a bilingual Sabbath School at 9:30, and an English church at 11:00. Those who had contributed to the worker fund became the main financial support and served as leaders of the English group. The congregation grew rapidly until they were able to purchase their own church, where it has continued to grow to this day.

> **"I have come into the world as a light, so that no one who believes in me should stay in darkness" (John 12:46).**

15. Russia Calling

It was a beautiful Sabbath morning in the fall of 1992. We were on our way to church and had the radio tuned to our local Adventist station. An announcement was made that that afternoon in a local church, there would be a speaker from the General Conference to share about the work in Russia. Communism had fallen the year before, and we were interested to find out how the work was going over there. Our Sabbaths were usually busy with visitation and church work, but this particular Sabbath, we had no plans, so decided to attend the meeting.

We sat about halfway back in the middle section of the church and listened as the speaker shared how the Lord had opened the way for a seminary, a press, and a medical center. We were thrilled with the stories he told. At some point the speaker said that they desperately needed a physician and a physical therapist for the medical center. I found myself sliding down in my seat as to avoid being seen. I was so active in our new church that I did not think that God would call us to Russia. I leaned over to Jeanie and said, "As soon as this is over, let's get out quick."

As we were walking out, someone pulled Jeanie aside to visit. I waited impatiently. Within two or three minutes, the speaker came directly up to me and said, "Hello, my name is Elder _____ (I can't remember his name now). What is your name and what kind of work do you do?"

I was caught. He told me that they desperately needed me in Russia. We told him we would pray about it. After much prayer, we felt that God was again calling us, this time to Russia. We told the conference that we would go.

In January, the General Conference sent us to their headquarters in Maryland for language study. There, we joined with the rest of the team that was going over next. Russian is a very hard language to learn, and we struggled with it. Our teacher was a non-Christian young lady who had recently moved from Russia. Jeanie and I didn't learn very much Russian, but we did have a chance to share the gospel with the teacher, who became quite annoyed with us.

In March of 1993, we packed, left our young adult children home, and headed for Moscow, Russia. The clinic was housed in an old abandoned orphanage that had been remodeled. As services, we offered physical therapy and dentistry. Half of our patients were Russians, and the other half were non-Russians working in Russia. The clinic was a success from the start, and the patients were happy with the care they received. We had trouble with the local government, who had promised us the building for free but was now asking for rent or new medical equipment. The director of the clinic, Dr. David Bowers, kept very busy dealing with the government issues and personnel problems.

> **The clinic was a success from the start, and the patients were happy with the care they received.**

When we arrived, we moved into a leased apartment that Dr. Bowers and his family lived in until the clinic was finished. We just got settled in and began our work, when we were notified that the apartment had been sold, and we would have to move. I protested that we still had more time on the lease. They responded that if we did not move, they would put our belongings out in the street. Housing was hard to find, and since the economy was so bad, two or three Russian families would move into one apartment and rent theirs at a high rate. We searched and finally found a man who would rent us his apartment. We packed our things and loaded them into an old military truck. When we arrived at the apartment, the man was dead drunk and had not moved out. The truck owner had to unload the truck that day, so our only option was to unload our things at the clinic and begin our search again. We lived in the physical therapy gym for several weeks before we found a vacant apartment.

Our new apartment was in a better location and was within walking distance of the clinic. We had great neighbors, some of whom spoke English. That was a real blessing and gave us the opportunity to share with them.

"And the peace of God, which transcends all understanding, will guard your hearts and your minds in Christ Jesus" (Phil. 4:7).

16. The Russian Mafia

After the fall of communism, many western companies began to move into Russia. These companies and their personnel were considered rich by the local people; therefore, mafia groups began to form and make threats if money was not paid for "protection." These generally were young men who claimed that if you paid, they would protect you from other mafia groups. The price was high. If payment was not received, they would destroy your buildings, cars, or even kill employees. The Russian president commissioned a taskforce to try to stop this but was not successful. Even some police worked as mafia during their off-duty time.

Jeanie, who was in charge of sterilization and cleanliness of the dental clinic, was walking through the upstairs area where the staff apartments were and met two young Russian men. She asked what they were doing in that area of the building. They said they were looking for the director. She told them that they had to go down to the office and make an appointment with Dr. Bowers' secretary. Dr. Bowers was available, so he had them meet him in the dining room. When Dr. Bowers arrived, there was only one man. The other one waited in the waiting area. As they visited, Dr. Bowers asked a lot of questions about what they were demanding. Suddenly, the young man looked toward the wall behind Dr. Bowers and began to shake and look very agitated. Dr. Bowers reached over, put his hand on his shoulder, and said, "Are you all right?" The man stood up and said that he had to go and fled the clinic with the other man. What did he see? Angel guards maybe?

The next day, Dr. Bowers received a call from the mafia "boss" who said, "Are you ready to pay?" Dr. Bowers replied that he was not ready to pay but was willing to talk. This same conversation continued on for several days, and then the boss began to make threats. Every morning as the staff met for worship, we prayed for protection. We sent emails to our friends asking for prayer, and soon we were receiving hundreds of responses, and we knew that the world-wide church was praying for us.

The clinic was surrounded by a fence, but we left the gate open during the day to allow patients to arrive. We had security guards at night. As the days went on, the threats continued, and we could see those two same young men walking outside of the gate, but they would never enter. At times, they would follow our personnel, but would never get close to them. We wondered if they were able to see angel guards all around us and the clinic. After a month or so, the threats stopped, and we never saw the same men again.

One of my patients was a pastor from another denomination. He and some young people had been doing some street evangelism when a mafia group came, stating that that corner of the street belonged to them and they had to pay fifty dollars. They paid. The next morning, the same guys came to the hotel where the pastor and his group were staying and asked to see the leader. When the leader came down, he was told that their boss had told them that they don't mess with God, and they returned the money! It is interesting how these young people steeped in atheism would even acknowledge that there is a God.

A few years later, I was serving as the director of the clinic, and another two young mafia men approached me. After the usual greetings, I asked them what they wanted. They asked, "Do you have protection?"

Knowing what they wanted and what they meant, I replied, "Yes." They then asked who we were getting protection from, and I pointed toward heaven and said, "God." They thanked me and left. That was the last time that we ever heard from a mafia group. God is great!

"The angel of the Lord encamps around those who fear him, and he delivers them" (Ps. 34:7).

17. War in Town

Following perestroika, many outside religions were infiltrating Russia. The Russian Orthodox Church highly opposed this and did all they could do to stop them from entering the country. In 1993 there were several Orthodox priests in the Duma, the legislative body of the government. These men were able to put a bill through to stop all foreign missionaries from entering Russia. The bill, along with a number of bills that he was opposed to, came across President Boris Yeltsin's desk to be signed. Mr. Yeltsin had three choices: to sign the bills and they would become law in which the West would be upset with him, to veto the bill in which his church leaders would be angry with him, or ignore the bills and they would become law after six months.

As we missionaries learned of this situation, we began to pray earnestly that God would kill the bill because it meant that all foreign missionaries would have to leave the country, and our work would be stopped. Mr. Yeltsin had been upset with the Duma for many reasons and did not want to sign these bills, so he decided to fire the Duma, which were housed in the "White House," comparable to our House of Congress. The Duma legislators refused to leave.

Early Monday morning, October 4, 1993, as I was having my devotional time, I heard a very loud rumbling sound coming from the street below. I pulled open the curtains and saw a number of military tanks and armored cars with troops, traveling toward the White House. Soon, we began to hear the sound of artillery fire. I turned on the Russian TV, but it was not broadcasting. We were concerned for our safety, as we had to walk to work. We had no idea what was happening. After prayer, we decided to proceed to the clinic, where we could learn the cause of the shelling.

When we arrived at the clinic, we were told that President Yeltsin had attacked the White House to roust out the Duma members. After the White House caught fire, the members left and the military departed. As a result, the bill was lost, and we were able to continue our work of leading people to Jesus. Again, God answered our prayers.

> **"Do not be afraid, little flock, for your Father has been pleased to give you the kingdom" (Luke 12:32).**

18. A New Church

In the latter part of 1993, evangelist Mark Finley came for the second time to Moscow to hold an evangelistic series. A large sports arena was rented for this event. During the series, the arena was packed. People were anxious to hear the Word of God. Bibles were in high demand. On a Friday evening, Elder Finley spoke on the Sabbath. He told the audience that, following the meeting, there would be placards placed around the arena that would identify the area in which the people lived. Eight theaters had been rented around the city of Moscow, and the persons holding the placard would instruct the people where the Sabbath services would be held the next day.

The next day, eight new churches were formed, some with nearly 1,000 attendees. An American pastor and a Russian pastor were assigned to each church. The theater near us was Ulan Bata, and we met there each Sabbath with our Russian people. Since we Americans still struggled with the language, we held an English Sabbath School class in the foyer of the theater. It was noisy as people came and went. Also, it was cold outside, so street vendors came in to stand behind the glass windows to sell their wares. We desired to be involved with the new church, but the language barrier was a problem.

Several weeks later, as I was walking to the clinic, I felt impressed that we needed to do something for our English-speaking patients. We were sharing Jesus with them during their treatment times, but we had no place to take them to church. I walked into Dr. Bowers' office and said that I thought we should hold services here in the clinic for our English-speaking patients. Dr. Bowers' eyes lit up, and he said that would be a great idea. He offered to teach the Sabbath School lesson. His secretary volunteered to play the piano, and the other physical therapist spoke up and said she would hold a class for the kids. We decided to start that next Sabbath.

The next Sabbath, about twelve people came to our sixty-seat lecture room, and since there was no one to do the sermon, I preached. During the next several months, our attendance increased until the lecture room was nearly full. About that time, the leader of the Adventist English School was doing an evangelistic series for the students. He asked our group to join them on Sabbaths and said that we would hold bilingual services. And so we did.

Each Friday evening, the school held a vesper service where there was singing, stories, and small group discussions on the Bible. The students could pick which subject they were interested in and go to that group. They loved it. At the end of the vesper service, it was announced that we would again have small groups meeting on the next day, Saturday. These would be our Sabbath School classes. The teachers at the school, most of them student missionaries from American Adventist colleges, taught the classes.

The church continued to grow. I started group baptismal classes and then received permission from the conference president to baptize. I kept telling the conference that they needed to assign a pastor to our church, but they always said, "You are the pastor." During the Sabbath School time, I liked to visit the classes to see how they were doing. I asked a young lady who had been coming for a while why she came. She replied with her head down that she came to learn English, but then, she raised her head, and with brightness in her eyes, said, "But now I have found God!" What a thrill that was for me.

> *I kept telling the conference that they needed to assign a pastor to our church, but they always said, "You are the pastor."*

Our church continued to grow until we had outgrown the 100-seat classroom. We then moved to a larger theater-type auditorium in the same building. It would hold 300 people. Unfortunately, the seats were theater-style and were fastened together in groups of four, and some were nailed to the floor. That arrangement did not work well for our small group Sabbath School discussion classes. Before we began on the first Sabbath in that auditorium, we were trying to figure out how we could move the chairs into a circle. One of us went over to a group of four chairs and lifted. It came right up, so we moved them into the shape of a triangle, so that we would have twelve seats per class. After Sabbath School was finished, they were slid back into place for the worship service.

Soon, we were having an attendance of around 200. The church was alive, and you could feel the Holy Spirit working. Most of the new members were young adults. Tithes and offerings began to pour in, and members were anxious to do their part. In fact, we never had a nominating committee. People just came forward and asked what they could do. One man came and said he lived near an orphanage and wanted to know if he could bring the kids. Some college students asked if they could start a ministry at their college by starting a midweek Bible study. One of our needs was someone to organize the music. We prayed about this, and the next week, a young couple with a small boy came to visit. I asked them what kind of work they did, and they replied that they were both music teachers. I asked if they would be willing to organize the music, and they were happy to do so. That was their first time in a Seventh-day Adventist church. They did a wonderful job as music coordinators, and after Bible studies, they were baptized.

As I visited with the attendees, I often asked how they liked the church. Their reply was always, "We like your church." We decided that it might be better to use as many as possible in our services: someone to say a prayer, another to translate the prayer, someone to call for the offering, and another one to translate, etc. Sometimes, we would have eighteen people on the platform. After starting this plan, when I asked the attendees, members or not, what they thought about the church they would reply, "We love our church."

I often prayed for the gift of tongues since the Russian language was just too difficult for me. The gift never really came, except in one incidence. Jeanie and I were visiting a member of our church. Her parents were visiting at that time, and we were introduced to them. They lived some distance away. He was an alcoholic as many of the men in Russia were at that time. While we were visiting, the church member was called away for a few minutes, and we were left alone with her parents. They could not speak English, and we could not speak much Russian. As we sat at the table, I felt impressed to share the gospel with them. But how? I sent up a prayer and began to speak in broken Russian and some English words. They listened. Soon tears were coming down their faces, and they understood. I never saw them again and pray that they gave their hearts to Christ permanently.

This was the most exciting time in my life. To witness the power of the Holy Spirit and to see lives changed was something many people never experience. I believe that the Holy Spirit is willing to work like this in all our churches today if we ask and pray earnestly for the Holy Spirit.

"If you then, though you are evil, know how to give good gifts to your children, how much more will your Father in heaven give the Holy Spirit to those who ask him!" (Luke 11:13).

19. The Sabbath Bus

Baptisms are always exciting. In Moscow we often had the baptisms in a large public swimming pool. All the churches would come together, and usually, a hundred or so candidates would be baptized. There would be ten or twelve pastors baptizing at the same time. It was a thrill to watch. One of the problems in having the baptisms in the public pools was that if the Orthodox Church heard of the location, they would threaten the keepers of the pool if they allowed us to use the facility. Because of this, it had to be a secret as to where it would be held. The candidates, members, pastors, and friends all had to go to a designated place to board buses that would take them to the pool.

During the summer, we usually tried to find a body of water for our baptisms. I found such a place on a walk one day. It was an old abandoned Pioneer Camp facility. This is similar to our Boy or Girl Scout camps. The buildings were run down, but there was a swimming pond with grassy slopes on the side. It looked like an ideal place for a baptism.

The day came for our next baptism. We planned to use the pond. It was a beautiful, warm Sabbath day, and the sun was bright. During the worship service, the four baptismal candidates were introduced and voted into membership subject to their baptism. It was announced that anyone who wanted to attend should meet in front of the auditorium and be led to a city bus that would take them to the pond.

Very few of the members or guests had cars, so everyone came on the metro or by bus to church. The clinic had a car that I would drive to the site and take the robes, blankets, etc. Jeanie would bring the people by bus. We didn't expect too many to attend, as it was lunch time. The bus that went by the pond was bus number seven. It was an old bus that seemed to have broken springs and an engine that needed replacing. All the busses on that route were in the same condition. The number seven bus usually came only every thirty minutes, if that. The bus would hold about fifty people and was always full.

At the end of the worship service, Jeanie went in front to meet the people who were going to the baptism. To her surprise, eighty people showed up. How was she going to get all those people onto bus number seven? As she led her flock to the bus stop, she prayed earnestly that God would help her. They waited as several other buses went by, and then came bus number seven. It was a brand-new bus with a trailer. There were no passengers on board. Wow! What a joy as they all got on the bus!

We lived on the same route as bus number seven, and for that year, we never saw that large bus again. The next summer, we planned to use the pond again, and sure enough, here came the big new bus again, but this time there were a few passengers on board. I wonder, does God make buses and send angels to drive them?

As I approached the pond with the car, I noticed on older gentleman setting his chair down on the grassy slope right where we would have the baptism. He got out his fishing pole and bait and began to fish. I didn't want to disturb him, but that was the only good place for our service. As the people came, they surrounded him and sat on the grass. He looked somewhat bewildered. One of the members explained to him what we were doing. He put his fishing gear aside and watched. After the baptism, I called for others who would like to study and prepare for baptism, and his hand went up. Praise the Lord for how He is working to save souls.

"Let us hold unswervingly to the hope we profess, for he who promised is faithful" (Heb. 10:23).

20. God Saved Me

I will call him Kent even though that is not his real name. Kent was a member of our International Church in Moscow. A smart, young engineering student, he was a spiritual leader and Sabbath School teacher. One Sabbath some of his friends reported to me that Kent was missing from the university and they had received a note saying something to the effect of: "I can't take it any longer." As we read the note we wondered if he had given up on his schooling and returned home or if this was indeed a suicide note. We had a special prayer of protection for Kent.

Over the next several days the students searched for Kent. Prayers went up throughout each day. It was discovered that he had moved to a different dorm room. He was not there but his belongings were in his room. It was wintertime so the concern was great.

Four days later Kent walked onto campus. His friends rejoiced to see him. All he could say was, "God saved me." The next day I sat down with Kent and he told me his story. As best as I can remember his story went like this:

> I have a problem. I have not been able to overcome a habit. I have been seeing a prostitute every week. It's always a different one each time. I have prayed and prayed for God to take this sin from me, but I could not stop. I was a hypocrite, so I decided to end my life.
>
> In my lab at school we have developed a very strong rat poison, so I put a large amount of the poison in my bag, bought a train ticket to the next country, and left. The next morning, I disembarked from the train, walked to a store, and purchased some strong vodka, then walked far into the country where I found an old abandoned house.
>
> I went into the house and drank the vodka to help me to stomach the rat poison. I ate all of the poison. I had no blanket. Two days later I woke up. I had no symptoms. God had saved me so here I am.

I prayed a prayer of thanksgiving to God for saving Kent. We then spent the next hour reviewing promises on how God gives us the victory through His Holy Spirit power. We read texts like Psalms 119:9–11: "How can a young person stay on the path of purity? By living according to your word. I seek you with all my heart; do not let me stray from your commands. I have hidden your word in my heart that I might not sin against you." We talked about the importance of spending much time in Bible study and prayer and fasting.

When Kent left he had joy—not only joy for God saving his life but joy in having the victory in Christ. Praise God for His mercy and power.

"I will give you a new heart and put a new spirit in you; I will remove from you your heart of stone and give you a heart of flesh" (Ezekiel 36:26).

21. Natasha

Eleven-year-old Natasha, blond hair, blue eyes, and a smile that would not quit, while rough-housing with her brother, fell and broke her forearm. She was taken to the emergency room where they applied a plaster cast without any padding or instructions concerning swelling, tingling of fingers, etc. Before the cast was removed, she had received damage to one of the three nerves in the forearm, giving her a partially disabled hand. The physicians tried to cut out the damaged part of the nerve and reattach it but without success. A second surgery was undertaken to transplant some tendons to give her better function. During that procedure, the surgeon accidentally cut a second nerve, leaving the hand nearly functionless.

Natasha came to our clinic for stretching exercises and help in adjusting to her disability. She could not speak any English, so

I had to communicate through a translator. The treatment was painful, but she never cried or grimaced. She just looked at me with those beautiful blue eyes and smiled no matter how hard I hurt her. After a few treatments, I began to share Jesus with her. When the translator asked her if she wanted to give her heart to Jesus, she replied in the affirmative. The translator/Bible worker then started Bible studies with Natasha and her mother. Soon they were attending church regularly.

After a few months, the Orthodox Church began to put articles in the newspaper against Seventh-day Adventists. They claimed that we would take their young people and never let them return home. They also claimed that we were sacrificing babies. This was a real concern for Natasha's parents, and soon, they forbade her to attend church. She came anyway. They took away her nice clothes, and she came in school clothes. They took away school clothes on the weekend, and she came in her work/play clothes. Then they locked the door so she could not leave, but when her father came home from work and forgot to lock the door, she escaped and attended the young people's meeting. Finally, the parents gave in and let her attend.

Then they locked the door so she could not leave, but when her father came home from work and forgot to lock the door, she escaped and attended the young people's meeting.

Natasha read the newspaper articles about Seventh-day Adventists and wrote a rebuttal article to the editor. It was not only published but the editor of the paper asked her to write weekly articles about her experience. In her science class at school, Natasha was learning about evolution, so she went to the teacher and told him that she believed in Creation. She presented herself in such a nice way that the teacher said he wanted to know more, so she shared the Bible Creation story with him.

A baptism was coming up, and Natasha wanted to be baptized. She told her parents what she was going to do. Again, out of fear, they threatened her with death if she proceeded to be baptized. The church and clinic staff prayed for Natasha to make the right decision and to be protected. We did not know what she would do, but on the evening of the baptism, Natasha showed up in her old clothes to be baptized. Coming up out of the water, I felt I could see the radiation of an angel on her face.

A short time later, Natasha was asked by the prayer coordinator to say the morning prayer during the worship service. When we assembled for prayer before the service, I had some concerns, as she was really a shy person. Could she pray in front of 200 people? I asked her if she was comfortable praying up front, and she replied yes. I was still somewhat concerned, so when we knelt for the prayer on the platform, I moved over closer to her in case she freaked out, and I could then take the mic and finish the prayer.

In the next few minutes, I experienced hearing the most beautiful prayer I have ever heard. She raised her disabled right hand and said, "Thank You for allowing me to have this injury because if it were not for this, I would not know Jesus. Thank You for Your wonderful salvation." She prayed for her family and for the church and that she could be an effective witness for Jesus. Most of us were in tears when she finished.

I never knew what happened to Natasha as her family moved away about the time we left Russia. I heard later that there was no Seventh-day Adventist Church where she lived, so she was attending the Baptist church. It is souls like this that I long to see again in heaven.

> **"Therefore, if anyone is in Christ, he is a new creation; the old has gone, the new has come!" (2 Cor. 5:17).**

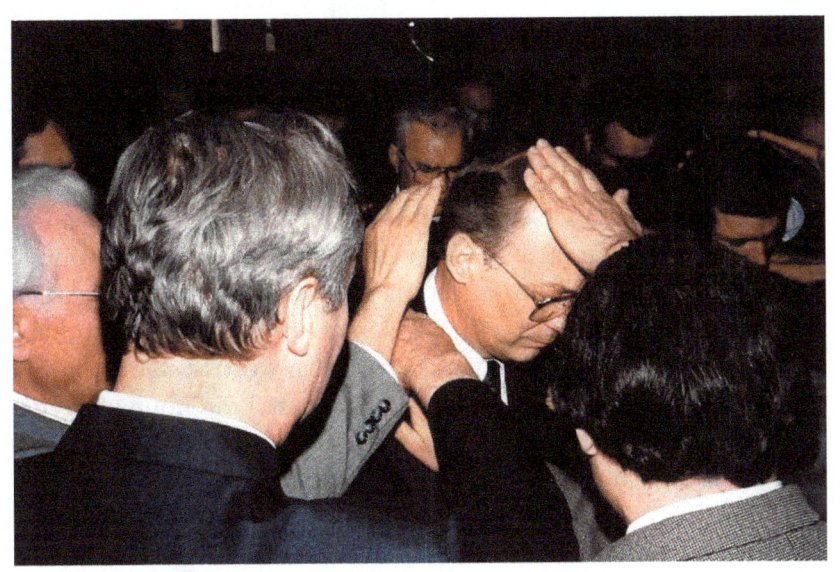

22. Ordination

When the church began to grow and services were more organized, I felt it was time to connect it to the local conference. The division office knew about our church, but I didn't think that the local conference did, so I asked my secretary to call the conference president and have him come to my office. When he came, I began to explain about our church, but he stopped me and said, "I know about the church. I have been there several times. Did you know that you have the most young people of any church in Moscow? Did you know that the church gave more tithes than all the other churches put together?" I sat there with my mouth open, shocked at the statistics. I had no knowledge of those things. He then asked me, "Are you blessed?"

"Yes," I replied, "I have been greatly blessed by what the Holy Spirit is doing in this church." He asked the same question again two more times, and I gave the same response. Finally, the interpreter turned to me and said that he was referring to ordination. I explained to him that I was a physical therapist and that I had not been ordained. He smiled and said they would look into that.

About one year later, I received a call from the division president, Elder Ted Wilson. He informed me that there was going to be an ordination service at the seminary in Zaokski and that I would be ordained. It is hard to express in words what I felt, but my feelings went like this: I am just a layman. I did not have a theology degree or seminary training. I am a physical therapist. How could I fill the role of a pastor? I felt so inadequate.

It was a beautiful spring Sabbath, April 20, 1996. We were assembled in the seminary chapel. The choir sang like angels, and we were blessed with Bible readings, special musical numbers, and challenging messages. The ordination followed with Elder Ted Wilson and his father, Elder Neal Wilson, conducting the service. Three pastors were set aside for the ministry of the gospel, including myself. What a blessing!! This was an exciting time yet a humbling experience for me.

> **"For this reason I remind you to fan into flame the gift of God, which is in you through the laying on of my hands. For God did not give us a spirit of timidity, but a spirit of power, of love and of self-discipline. So do not be ashamed to testify about our Lord ... who has saved us and called us to a holy life—not because of anything we have done but because of his own purpose and grace" (2 Tim. 1:6–9).**

23. Burnout

When one is a missionary, they often take on more responsibility than they can handle. I am one of those. I tend to see things that need to be done and do it myself until I burn out. In Russia it was no different. I was called to Russia to be a physical therapist. When we arrived, I was given the responsibility to be the assistant director of the clinic. Later, I perceived that we were not living up to the name "Adventist Health Center of Moscow." We were not doing any health classes to teach the people about a healthier way of life, so I began to hold weekly health classes. As time when on, the dental section realized that I had some mechanical skills, so I was elected to replace bearings in the drills, fix the leaking hydraulic cylinders in the dental chairs, and keep the x-ray machine going; all this in addition to being a full-time physical therapist.

Then, I became the pastor of our growing congregation. Then, the other PT became very ill and had to be sent home to England. Later, the director of the clinic took a permanent return to the USA. I was put in as the director, a full-time job, against my will. One day, visitors from the General Conference arrived and wanted a tour. Suddenly, I felt the pressure increasing, and I began to feel pain from my left jaw down into my left arm. I feared that I was having a heart attack. I sent up a quick prayer, "God, I don't have time for a heart attack now. Please help me." The pain subsided.

> *Suddenly, I felt the pressure increasing, and I began to feel pain from my left jaw down into my left arm. I feared that I was having a heart attack.*

After not being able to get any help, I closed the physical therapy department and focused on keeping the other aspects of the clinic running. Still, my body was giving me warning signs, chest pain. My wife, Jeanie, and I prayed for help, but God answered in a different way. I received an email from the Hawaii Conference inviting me to be a pastor there. Wow! What a nice place to heal. I trained a Russian lady, who had been with us since the beginning, as an administrator and accepted the invitation to Hawaii.

We packed our belongings and flew home to California to spend a few days with our children; then on to Hawaii. The change in climate and having only one job as a pastor was refreshing. God blessed me and my ministry.

For the first several years, we lived in the parsonage near the church. As we looked toward the future, we really wanted to retire in Hawaii. There was one problem. Housing was extremely expensive. Older homes were selling for more than $600,000, depending on their location. We knew that would be impossible.

Then 9/11 happened, and the prices dropped. Since many military personnel had to leave for overseas duty, there were many foreclosures. A friend showed us a nice house not far from the beach. It had four bedrooms, three full bathrooms, and was located on a nice corner lot. The yard was fully landscaped. We contacted the realtor, who told us to make a bid as the bank had not set a price yet. This called for prayer. What was God's plan? After praying, I felt impressed to offer the ridiculous price of $180,000. The bank accepted it the same day! Another miracle from our precious Lord.

"God is not unjust; he will not forget your work and the love you have shown him as you have helped his people and continue to help them" (Heb. 6:10).

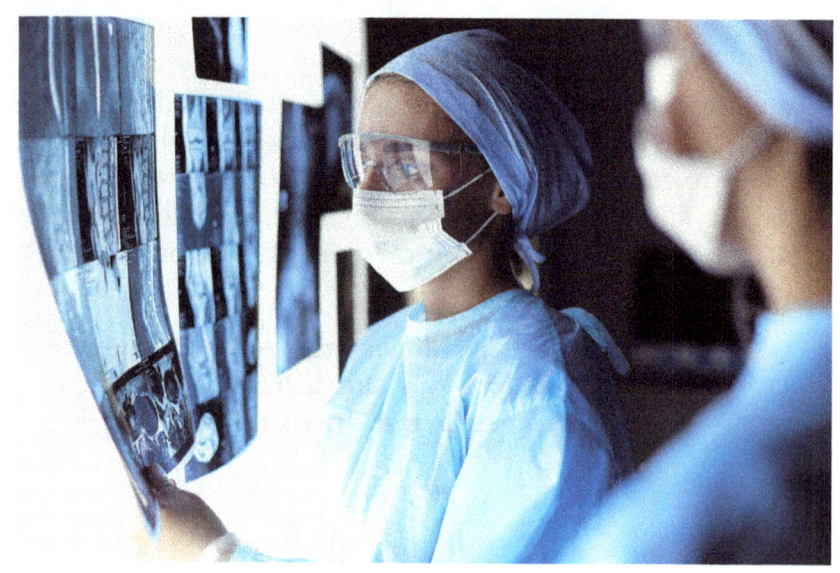

24. The Big "C" Word

Not long after arriving in Moscow, Jeanie felt a lump in her left breast. At that time, Russian medicine was inadequate. We elected to return to the USA and see our family doctor. When we arrived in California, we were able to get an appointment the next day. The doctor examined Jeanie and was quite certain that this was cancer. He ordered a mammogram and a biopsy. God was with us and allowed us to get those tests done the next day. It was cancer. It's hard to express the feelings one experiences when that "C" word is mentioned. It is scary. We prayed for guidance.

Jeanie opted for modified radical breast mastectomy. The surgery was performed the next week. No lymph nodes were involved, so it was felt that her prognosis was very good. On Sabbath forty friends came to visit her. This was very encouraging. She was sent home after a few days for recovery. About one week later, the stress of cancer and surgery caught up with her emotionally. She began to cry over little things and was having difficulty coping. We returned to the doctor's office. He explained that she had had an emotional overload, and that she needed to be on some antidepressants for a short time.

We spent time with the kids and grandkids and other relatives. We also consulted with some specialists on natural ways to prevent further flare-ups. After a few weeks, we headed back to Russia. Her health stabilized and she was able to work in the dental office as an assistant. She remained cancer-free for the next eleven years.

One morning in 2003, Jeanie asked me to feel something under her left arm. I could feel a lump about the size of my thumb. Again we consulted with the doctor, who ordered a biopsy. We were not able to get the appointment with the pathologist for several weeks. In the meantime, Jeanie decided on the advice of a friend to go on a raw food diet. She bought some raw food cookbooks and began her new eating regime. We even had friends, Josué and Ruth Rosado (principal and wife of Hawaiian Mission Academy), over for a raw food Thanksgiving dinner. It was amazingly delicious. When she finally saw the pathologist for the biopsy, the lump was the size of a pea. The doctor had to have me find it for him, as it was so small. He advised to continue doing what she had been doing and leave it alone, but Jeanie wanted it out. An ultrasound was used, so the doctor could guide the biopsy needle to that small lump. The pathology report—Positive.

Surgery was arranged to remove the involved lymph node. When the surgeon went in to take out the node, he found it entwined in the brachial plexus, the nerves that go into the arm. Because of this, he had to cut the node to get it out. Unfortunately, the cut open node spread the viruses and soon lesions were showing up in various places. A few months later, x-rays revealed that the cancer had spread to the bones. She started some mild chemotherapy.

Prior to the onset of cancer, Jeanie had a fear of suffering with pain. Her spiritual life also suffered. She was a pastor's kid and grew up feeling that if she did all the right things, she would be okay. When the big "C" word came, she was devastated. At first, she questioned, "Why me," then suffered mild depression. After the second surgery, her attitude and spiritual life changed. She began to study the Word deeply and spend time alone with God. She started a women's group at church to teach women how to have a deep relationship with God. She even was a speaker at the conference women's retreat; something she would never had done before. Now, instead of crying or complaining when she had pain, she would sing, pray, and read the Bible. It was exciting to watch her grow spiritually.

In early March 2005, Jeanie was experiencing pain in her right hip. She had been working in her flowerbed, so we felt that she had strained some muscles. She was having trouble walking, so I got a walker for her to use around the house. The next Sabbath, she decided to stay home because of the pain. I had a very busy day of preaching, potluck, and afternoon meetings. During the dinner, one of the teens borrowed my cell phone and returned it in the off mode. At home Jeanie was going up the stairs to her room when she fell on the landing halfway up. She was able to crawl up the rest of the stairs to my office with the intent to call me. When she reached up for the desk phone, it fell on her breaking her glasses. She was finally able to call, but my phone was off without my knowledge. She managed to get herself into bed, and when I arrived, that evening she was smiling and said, "You will never guess what happened to me today. It was really funny." I was amazed she could be so happy after all that pain.

I examined her hip, and I was certain that it was broken. I called her doctor, but he was not available. I finally got her into the car and to the hospital emergency room. The x-rays demonstrated that she did have a fractured hip due to cancer. Surgery was scheduled for the next day. I called our kids, and they insisted on flying over to Hawaii to be with Jeanie. After the surgery, Jeanie had a hard time getting over the anesthesia. After a couple of days, the doctor informed her that the other hip was about to break, and that he wanted to put a pin in it to stabilize it. Jeanie did not want another surgery because of the after effects of the anesthesia. The doctor said it was only a twenty-minute procedure with only a light anesthesia. Finally, she decided to go again into surgery.

The surgery lasted for hours, and when she came out, she was on a ventilator and taken to the critical care unit. We were told that she probably would not live. We prayed. I wanted her to live, but I did not want her to continue to have pain and eventually die from the cancer. The surgeon never told us what happened, so I called the anesthesiologist. He told me that the surgeon decided to put a rod down her entire femur bone. He did not have the correct size for her small bones, so decided to drill out the marrow of the bone. There is an abundance of blood vessels there and the drilling infiltrated air into her vascular system, which went to her lungs causing her to stop breathing.

Jeanie passed to her rest on March 13, 2005. This was a bitter/sweet experience. Bitter because I would miss the bride of my youth, and for the kids, the loss of a mother. Sweet because now she would no longer suffer the pain associated with cancer. She was safe and ready for Jesus to come. That gave me encouragement and peace.

> **"For men are not cast off by the LORD forever. Though he brings grief, he will show compassion, so great is his unfailing love" (Lam. 3:31–32).**

25. Remarriage

They say that when a wife loses her husband, her first thoughts are, how shall I survive. When a man loses his wife, his prime concern is where can I find another good wife. I certainly can identify with the latter. I suppose that most of my grieving was done long before her death, knowing that an early death was a probability. Also, as a Christian, and believing that soon Jesus would return and all would be restored, helped me "not to grieve like the rest of men, who have no hope" (1 Thess. 4:13).

A month or so after Jeanie's death, her brother, David, suggested that I get reacquainted with Jewell. I had known Jewell's husband in academy. Several years after academy, Jewell's husband and I were inducted into the US Army about the same time. By that time, we were both married. Jewell and her husband lived near us while in the service. Later, we moved to Wisconsin, where our friends the Conners lived. In time, we found out that Mrs. Conner was Jewell's sister, and when the two families got together, we were invited. Jewell's husband passed away in 2003.

I asked David for an address or phone number for Jewell, but he was unable to supply that information. A few weeks later, David and his wife went to Michigan to visit their daughter. While there, he visited one of his grade school students, Jewell's son, Greg, who was attending the seminary at Andrews University. David asked Greg how his mother was and if she planned to remarry. He replied that she was doing well but had no intentions to remarry. Greg also stated that they were praying that she would find someone to be a helpmeet for her. David suggested my name. The next weekend, Greg invited his major professor home for dinner. The professor's wife is my first cousin. Over dinner my name came up, and the matchmaking began. The professor obtained Jewell's address, phone number, cell phone number, email, her work address, and her work phone number from Greg. The professor sent this all to me.

Greg called his mother and asked her if she remembered me, and if she knew that Jeanie had passed away. She remembered me but did not know about Jeanie's death. He suggested to her that I might be sending her an email. She doubted it. The next day she received my first email.

After emailing for several months, I finally got up enough courage to call her, and wow—that beautiful, sweet voice just overwhelmed me! We talked about many things; things about our work, our children, and times in the army. We prayed together before hanging up.

In August Jewell told me that her son, Greg, and family, and her daughter and family were coming to be with her for a week and that she was going to take that week off from her work. I invited her and her family to come to Hawaii for a vacation. After considering that, it was decided that it would be too expensive, so she declined my invitation. When that week came, I was having breakfast with David and Helen, his wife. Helen suggested that I should go to Oregon and meet Jewell and her family. David interjected the thought that the airfare to the mainland at that time was very expensive, probably about $1,300. There were two problems with the suggestion. First, it was too expensive, and second, Jewell had not invited me, and I knew she was too shy to do that.

As I walked home on that beautiful Sunday mid-morning, I began praying about Jewell and our relationship. What was God's plan? If this was not His plan, I didn't want to continue the relationship for fear of hurting Jewell, and if it was God's plan, I needed to know how to proceed. I prayed, "Lord, if it is Your plan that I continue this relationship, and if I should go to Oregon to see her, please give me a sign. In fact, give me two signs. One, help me find a ticket for under $500 and two, have her invite me."

> "LORD, *if it is Your plan that I continue this relationship, and if I should go to Oregon to see her, please give me a sign.*

When I got home, I brought up the Hawaiian Airline website. A big full-screen ad pushed itself into my face—$398 round trip to Portland, Oregon. The hair on the back of my neck stood up, and goosebumps appeared on my arms. That's number one!

Jewell was home baking and preparing for the coming of the kids. She kept hearing this inaudible voice saying, "Invite Vernon, invite Vernon." She struggled with that and thought of reasons why she couldn't do that. She wondered what the family would think, and she was too bashful. Finally, after hearing this voice over and over, she washed her hands, went to her computer, and sent me an email saying, "Why don't you come over here?" Wow! That was number two, all within fifteen minutes of my talk with God.

I made the reservations for that Wednesday. I bought leis for all the ladies, toys for the kids, and gifts for the guys and left for Oregon. When I arrived, I was greeted warmly. The oldest grandson wasn't sure about having a future step-grandfather, but even he was excited to have me there. Jewell served cherry pie after dinner. I was told that it was a family tradition that if anyone had a cherry pit in their pie, they got to kiss the cook. Unfortunately, I didn't get one, and neither did anyone else. I offered twenty dollars for anyone to give me a cherry pit. After a few minutes, the grandson came in with a cherry pit he had found under the neighbor's cherry tree. The look on his face when I kissed his grandmother was priceless and worth the twenty dollars! Over those few days, Jewell and I went out to eat, walked in the parks, and enjoyed her family.

At the end of September, Jewell came to Hawaii and stayed with David and Helen. We had a wonderful time together. I made arrangements with a very nice hotel on the beach to make a special vegetarian dinner for us. After eating, we walked down on the beach at sunset. It was a beautiful setting. I stopped and faced Jewell and asked, "Will you marry me?" Her reply—yes! We were married on February 12, 2006, in a beautiful garden overlooking the ocean.

I had intended to continue in my ministry for at least another year when I would be old enough to retire. Jewell did not want to live in Hawaii and wanted to live near her children. As we were considering our options, I lost my voice and was unable to preach for several weeks. It seemed that God was telling us to retire, and so we both retired and moved to her home in Oregon. Since that time, God has blessed us financially, spiritually, and our marriage has been wonderful.

> **"Enjoy life with your wife, whom you love, all the days of this meaningless life that God has given you under the sun—all your meaningless days. For this is your lot in life and in your toilsome labor under the sun" (Eccles. 9:9).**

26. Retirement

Working folk often look forward to retirement. There were times that I did, but I guess like any other time in life, it has its advantages and disadvantages. I'll share with you the good and the bad (which often turned out for good). As a pastor, you always have a burden for others who don't know Jesus. So, even in retirement, you continue to work for the Lord, only without pay, of course.

When we left Hawaii, we were able to sell our house for a very good price. This provided us with funds to invest in rentals that God has blessed us with and which we could use to support students and missions. After moving into Jewell's home, it just didn't feel like it was my home. This led to a remodeling of her house. I removed walls that separated the living room, dining room, family room, and entryway. We put in all new doors and repainted the whole inside. It then felt like my home also.

After getting settled, we became active in the church, which meant going to elder's meetings, business meetings, board meetings, prayer meetings, and work bees, in addition to teaching a Sabbath School class and occasionally preaching. The church that we were attending did not seem to grow much, so the pastor called on the congregation to have ten days of prayer. We met every night for ten days, praying for the church, its members, and the community. The results were amazing. We began to have more and more visitors, including community folk. The church grew to the point that we had to start a second service. Prayer really works!

In 2008 we joined Share Him Seminars and went to Madagascar to preach evangelistic meetings. That was a wonderful experience. The hall that the church rented was packed every night, with around 750 people. God really blessed, and there were many baptisms. During our stay there, we were able to visit the forest where the lemurs lived. They are interesting creatures. We fed them bananas, and most were very friendly and would swing from tree to tree and back down to get another handout.

Several evenings the electricity went out, so my computer and projector would not work as well as there was no amplification system, but with the Lord's help, we continued. On about the fifth night, my computer refused to work. The locals said that it had received a virus, and it would take several days to get it fixed. One night, after the meeting was over, we got together with the other evangelists to compare notes. One of the men said that his slides were in the Romanian language. Others said the same thing. There was one young man who was preaching in a small country church who had never had any preaching experience. I noticed that he spent a lot of time in prayer. That night he said his slides were in Malagasy, the local language. We turned on his computer and brought up his slides, and, lo and behold, they were in Romanian. God had miraculously changed the screen to be in Malagasy. That was the same night that I preached without a computer, so I was also blessed as my CD also was in Romanian. What a great God we have!

One Sunday evening, we came to the meetings and found the congregation all standing on the outside of the building. We learned that there was a wedding reception going on in the hall. Someone went in and told the person in charge that we had rented the hall and that we needed to start our meetings. They refused and said that they would not leave. The pastor and several elders met in the parking lot, knelt down, and prayed. After a few minutes, the person in charge came out and said they had decided to leave. We all jumped in and helped them with the cleanup and then took down the tables and set the chairs in place. When we are about God's work, He holds back the adversary to make way for the gospel to go forward.

My interpreter's name was Neat. He did a fantastic job of translating. He was a college graduate and still single, but he desired to be an evangelist. He had been preaching in the nearby churches and had even translated one of E.G. White's books into Malagasy. His education was not in theology, so the conference did not want to hire him as a Bible worker. We became good friends. After we returned home, we continued our relationship with him through email. Jewell and I prayed that there might be some way that he could get into the ministry. We explored options with him. Finally, with the Lord's help, we were able to get him into the seminary at Andrews University. He studied hard and graduated with an M.Div. degree. Now he is serving as a pastor, has married a lovely girl, and they have two beautiful children. This was a real blessing to us, and we feel like they are part of our family.

Following our series in Madagascar, we took a side trip to northern South Africa to Krueger Park, a huge wildlife refuge. What a thrill that was to be out with God's creatures, see their habitats, and to learn about each creature from our guide. We saw hundreds of animals. We saw many interesting fowl, along with lions, elephants, giraffes, leopards, hippopotamus, cape buffalos, monkeys, and many others. One elephant became curious and poked his nose into our open truck to check us out! We were able to stay near the park for three nights and go into the park every day. What a thrill that was. I long for heaven where all those beautiful animals will be tame.

In late 2011 the big "C" word popped up again; this time, prostate cancer. I elected to go to Loma Linda University Medical Center's proton treatment. It was a great program and quite spiritual. There was plenty of time to share with the other patients, who were very worried and afraid. We were there for three months, with treatments five times per week. Some very close friends of ours had moved from Loma Linda but had left their furniture and food in the house. They graciously let us live there without any charge; another wonderful blessing from God and friends.

Unfortunately, my cancer came back in 2017. There were few options for treatment since I couldn't have any more radiation, and since the proton radiation causes a lot of scar tissue, surgery was not a possibility. The only option was to have cryosurgery, a procedure to freeze the prostate. Something went wrong in surgery, and my urethra, the urinary tube that goes through the prostate, was severely damaged. After the urethral and super pubic catheters were removed, I experienced severe pain during urination, so the catheters were replaced. This went on for months. Finally, the catheters were removed, and the pain had subsided. Then a new problem arose. The urine was escaping into my groin, out my rectum, and going down under the skin of my right leg. It was then decided to do a surgery to remove the bladder, prostate, etc., and do an ileostomy, a procedure to reroute the urine to a bag on my side, after which I began to heal. This situation was over many months, and several hospital stays. During that time, I was able to share Jesus with nurses, doctors, and other hospital staff. I will share a couple of those stories.

Erin was a delightful nurse and very caring. She came to my room often, and we talked a lot. As I was nearing discharge, she asked me about driving home. I told her we would not leave until Sunday. She explained that traffic in Portland was very heavy on Friday but that Saturday was a good time to go. Impressed by the Holy Spirit, I asked her if she knew that Saturday was the Lord's Day. She looked at me with a curious stare and finally asked if I was a Seventh-day Adventist. I answered in the affirmative. She then admitted that she had been raised a Seventh-day Adventist. I asked her what happened. She replied that after going away to school, she just quit going to church but that she really needed to go back. I asked her if Jesus would come that night, would she go to heaven. She didn't know. I shared the gospel with her and asked her if she wanted to receive Jesus Christ into her heart and have the assurance of salvation. She said yes, and we prayed together, and she gave her heart to the Lord. Afterward, I asked her again that if Jesus were to come that night, would she go to heaven. She exclaimed YES! and jumped around the room and gave me a big hug. There is nothing better in life than to lead someone to Jesus.

> *There is nothing better in life than to lead someone to Jesus.*

That same night, an aide came in to take my vitals. He had an accent, so I asked him where he was from. He said he was from Tibet. We talked a little about the political situation there; then I asked him if he was Buddhist. He was. We talked briefly about the comparison between Buddhism and Christianity. I mentioned that Buddha was dead, but Jesus Christ was alive. He said he knew that and wanted to study the Bible.

Unfortunately, he had to continue to see his patients, so our conversation was cut short, but as he was leaving the room, I said, "Just remember, Jesus loves you."

He turned to me and said, "This I know, for the Bible tells me so." I pray that he will continue to study and give his heart to the Lord.

Some of the other staff shared some of their life problems, and I was able to share and pray with them. So you see that a bad situation can turn into a blessing to lead people to trust in Jesus.

I have been involved in prison ministry for about twenty-one years. At one prison in Hawaii, there was a program called "Spilling Your Guts." It allows prisoners to tell whatever they want to a chaplain. Some just want to get something "off their chest," or are looking for repentance and forgiveness, or discussing family problems. One man came to me and admitted that he had killed another person even though he was never convicted for that crime. He was incarcerated for selling drugs. I had the wonderful privilege to lead him to Christ and begin Bible studies. I gave him a Bible and a couple of lessons to study, and I returned the next week.

When I saw him again, he said, "As I was reading the Bible, I saw that the Sabbath was on the seventh day and not the first day."

I told him he was right and asked if he had ever been acquainted with a Seventh-day Adventist. He told me that he had never heard of them. We finished the lessons, and he was discharged. About six months later, he entered into the baptistery and surrendered his life fully to the Lord.

As I write this, I am involved in prison ministry at the Washington State Penitentiary. We have more than forty volunteers going in each week to preach, teach, and counsel. Right now, I am conducting a class for a few men who would like to become pastors when they are released. It's a class I call Practical Ministry. These men love to study the Bible and share with other prisoners. What a joy to work with them.

This last summer, on the way to camp meeting and pulling our fifth wheel RV, I rear-ended a pickup in front of me who had suddenly stopped, and I had nowhere to go. We are thankful that no one was hurt, but our pickup was totaled. The other driver was a Christian man and was very nice. I was really happy about that. After clearing the highway, I rode with the tow truck driver, and Jewell rode with the ODOT (Oregon Department of Transportation) man. We both were able to share Jesus with both of these men. The tow truck took our truck to their lot and then pulled our partially damaged trailer to the camp meeting. We had a wonderful time at the camp meeting, and a friend pulled our trailer home for us. Then God provided a nice, new pickup for us.

During the process of buying the new pickup, we discovered that the young salesman had been raised a Seventh-day Adventist. We shared Jesus with him and encouraged him to return to church. Also, when we went to another office to sign papers, we met a young mother who was raised a Catholic. As we visited and shared, she told us that she had been reading her Bible and that she discovered that Saturday was the true Lord's day. We were surprised. Then she also said that she had discovered that people do not go to heaven or hell when they die but stay in the grave until Jesus comes. I asked her if she would like some Bible study guides, and she said yes. After arriving home, I sent her a set of lessons. We pray that she follows through with them. So you see that there are always opportunities to share, in the bad times and in the good times.

> **"He is like a tree planted by streams of water, which yields its fruit in season and whose leaf does not wither. Whatever he does prospers" (Ps. 1:3).**

27. Frustration Turns to Joy

I had just spent five wonderful days in southern California with my kids and relatives for Thanksgiving. My flight home was broken up into three segments. Now, tired and cold, I waited for the shuttle to transfer me to another terminal for the last leg home. Finally, the shuttle came but had to wait for one more passenger. Soon, a young woman in her late twenties boarded the shuttle, and we proceeded to the terminal. After getting checked in for the final flight, I sat down, and the young lady sat near me. We greeted each other. Her name was Maggie. She worked for FEMA and was on her way to the county seat to lecture on disaster readiness.

As we were gathering our belongings to be ready for boarding, an announcement came over the intercom that our flight had been canceled due to freezing fog. Now what? I approached the desk and asked if there would be a flight out the next day and was told that there was no way to get out until two days later. The only solution was to rent a car and drive the four-and-a-half hours to where my car was parked at the airport. Was I too tired to drive that far? Should I wait until tomorrow? Maggie was on her phone. When she hung up, I suggested that we rent a car together. She replied that she had already rented one, and I was welcome to join her. That was great—she would drive.

As we traveled through rain and fog, we talked, sharing different turns in our lives. I shared how God had worked in my life, and she told me that she was interested in religion but did not go to a church. I asked her if Jesus came tonight would she go to heaven. She was somewhat taken back and really didn't know. I then shared the gospel with her, and when I finished, she said, "Count me in!" I was thrilled. She then asked many questions about God, the Bible, and the Seventh-day Adventist Church. That conversation lasted the rest of the trip. As we departed, I encouraged her to continue her study of the Bible and to get to know Jesus in a real way. She agreed and left happy.

My frustration had turned to joy!

> **"Yet I am always with you; you hold me by my right hand. You guide me with your counsel, and afterward you will take me into glory" (Ps. 73:23–24).**

TEACH Services, Inc.
P U B L I S H I N G

We invite you to view the complete
selection of titles we publish at:
www.TEACHServices.com

We encourage you to write us
with your thoughts about this,
or any other book we publish at:
info@TEACHServices.com

TEACH Services' titles may be purchased in
bulk quantities for educational, fund-raising,
business, or promotional use.
bulksales@TEACHServices.com

Finally, if you are interested in seeing
your own book in print, please contact us at:
publishing@TEACHServices.com
We are happy to review your manuscript at no charge.

www.ingramcontent.com/pod-product-compliance
Lightning Source LLC
Chambersburg PA
CBHW070558160426
43199CB00014B/2547